How We Used to Live

Memories of
GOING TO WORK

By Ruth Owen

Published in 2025 by **Ruby Tuesday Books Ltd.**

Copyright © 2025 **Ruby Tuesday Books Ltd.**

All rights reserved. No part of this publication may be reproduced in whole or in part, stored in any retrieval system, or transmitted in any form or by any means, electronic, mechanical, photocopying, recording, or otherwise, without written permission from the publisher.

Editor: Mark J. Sachner
Design & Production: Emma Randall

Photo credits:
Alamy: 6 (Alice Mitchell), 8 (Hum Images), 9 (Sueddeutsche Zeitung Photo), 11 (The Print Collector), 12T (thislife pictures), 13B (thislife pictures), 14 (Smith Archive), 19T (Allan Cash Picture Library), 20B (Trinity Mirror/Mirrorpix), 21C (Dave Bagnall Archive), 22 (Barry Lewis), 23R (Trinity Mirror/Mirrorpix); iStock Photo: 5BR (Grafissimo), 12B (vandervelden); Public Domain: 18L, 19B, 23L; Ruby Tuesday Books: 7B, 15; Shutterstock: Cover (Sergiy1975/Iantapix/OddMary/marekuliasz/Ivan Smuk), 4L, 4R (Anwarul Kabir Photo), 5L (Howard Double), 5TR (marekuliasz), 7B (Dr Morley Read), 10 (Krasowit/Anwarul Kabir Photo/OddMary/Clara Bastian), 13T (Evan Lorne/Afonkin_Y/Andre Devereux/Dejan Dundjerski/New Africa/BW Folsom), 18R (marekuliasz), 20T (Sarah2), 21T (Jiang Hongyan/Bborriss.67/Chinh Truc), 21B (Ivan Chistyakov); Superstock: Cover & 1 (4x5 Collection/Devaney Collection), 7T (Underwood Photo Archive), 16 (H. Armstrong Roberts/ClassicStock), 17 (4x5 Collection/Devaney Collection).

British Library Cataloguing in Publication Data (CIP) is available for this title.

ISBN: 978-1-78856-422-9

Printed in Poland by L&C Printing

www.rubytuesdaybooks.com

CONTENTS

Looking into the Past 4

Making Bricks 6

Organ Grinders 8

Delivering the Milk 10

Hardworking Shopkeepers 12

Telegram Boys 14

Number, Please! 16

Making Words 18

Rag-and-Bone Men 20

Hold Very Tight, Please! 22

Glossary, Index, Answers 24

LOOKING INTO THE PAST

This book is all about the work that people in Britain used to do in the **past**.

Using **historical** photographs and objects from the 1900s, we will find out about different jobs.

We will also hear the real-life **memories** of people who lived in the 1900s, or 20th Century.

Together, photos, objects and memories can help us learn about history.

**Look at the photos on these pages.
How do you think people used these objects at work?**
(The answers are inside the book and on page 24.)

What Is a Century?

We measure history in periods called **centuries**.
A century lasts for 100 years. Today, we are in the 21st Century.

1801 to 1900	**1901 to 2000**	**2001 to 2100**
19th Century	20th Century	21st Century

Many of the photos in this book are from a time that we call "living history". It's a time that people who are still alive today can remember.

MAKING BRICKS

In the late 1800s and early 1900s, a whole family might work at their town's brickworks.

To make a brick, a worker packed wet clay into a mould using their hands.

The shaped bricks were then removed from their moulds and left to dry in the air for several weeks. Finally, the bricks were baked inside a large oven called a kiln.

The heavy bricks were pushed to and from the kilns in barrows.

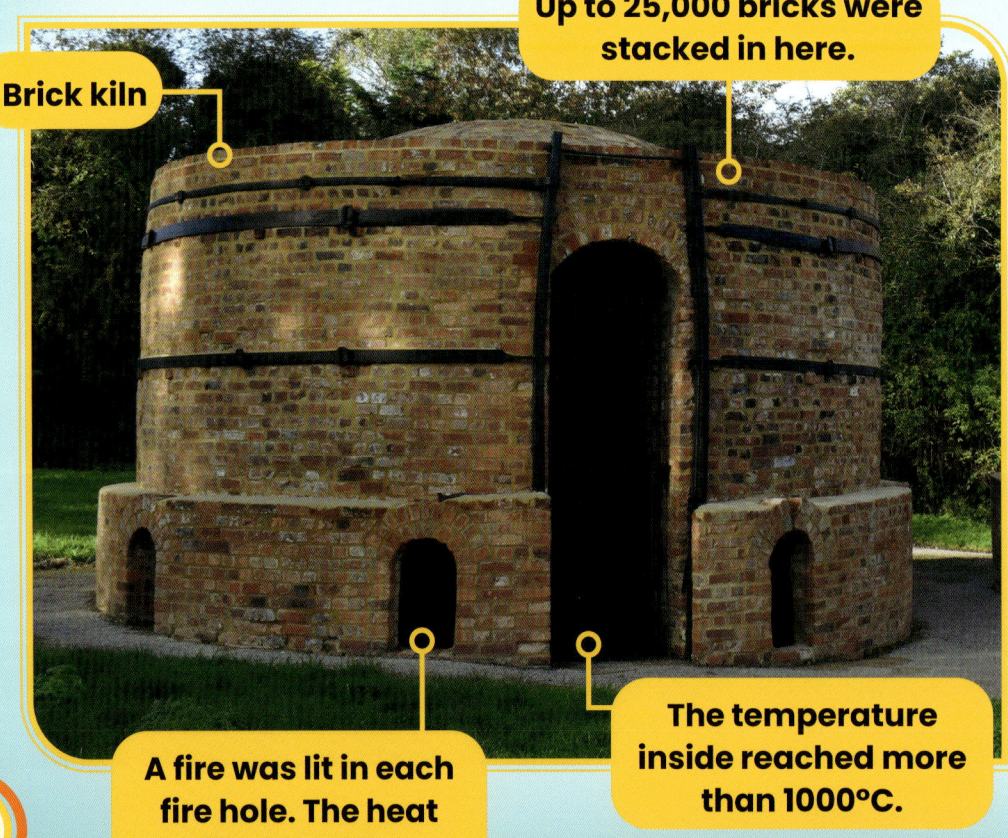

Brick kiln

Up to 25,000 bricks were stacked in here.

A fire was lit in each fire hole. The heat filled the kiln.

The temperature inside reached more than 1000°C.

A brickworks in the 1930s

Bricks

Barrow

In the 1900s, some brickworks began to use machinery. Workers who still made bricks in the old way were proud of their work. They would make a thumbprint in each wet brick to show it was handmade.

This brick's mould showed where the brick was made.

Wooden brick mould

ORGAN GRINDERS

In the early 1900s, you might have heard music coming from a barrel organ played by an organ grinder.

People living in poverty had no radios or other ways to hear music.

When an organ grinder came to their street, they would leave their homes to listen and even dance.

Organ grinders often had a monkey that was trained to collect money from the audience.

Today, we know it is very cruel to take a monkey from its wild forest home and make it do work.

The monkey was kept on a lead.

The organ grinder turned a handle that pumped air through the organ, so it played a tune.

Organ grinder

Barrel organ

The barrel organ could play about six different tunes.

DELIVERING THE MILK

Today, most people buy their milk in bottles or cartons.

In the 1800s and early 1900s, milk was delivered to homes in metal churns.

The churns of milk were carried by horse and cart from **local** farms to a village or town's **dairy**.

Milkmen and milkwomen, who worked for the dairy, loaded the heavy churns onto handcarts. Then they pushed the carts from house to house.

Milk churn

Milk measure

Customer's jug

Customer · Milkman · Churn · Two-wheeled handcart

John (Born 1940)

"My nan was our village's milk woman. Early each morning, she pushed her handcart from the dairy to her customers to deliver milk for their breakfasts. No one had a fridge in those days, and in hot weather, milk quickly went off. So Nan also made a second delivery of fresh milk in the afternoon. She must have walked miles!"

The customer asked for an amount of milk. Then the milkman or milkwoman scooped it from the churn with a measure and poured it into the customer's own jug.

HARDWORKING SHOPKEEPERS

Before there were self-service supermarkets, people bought **groceries** from small local shops.

A grocery shop in 1924 (Shopkeeper)

At a grocery shop, customers patiently queued.

When they reached the front of the queue, they read out their shopping list. Then the shopkeeper fetched each item for them.

Vegetables and other goods were weighed on scales.

As a shopkeeper weighed and wrapped goods, they chatted to their customers, sharing news and local gossip.

Flour, sugar and tea were scooped from large sacks, weighed and put into paper bags. Foods such as bacon, cheese and butter were wrapped in paper – there was no plastic packaging!

Bacon was sliced with a knife.

Bacon slab

Bacon rashers

Cheese was cut from a large block with a cheese wire.

Glass jars of sweets

A shopkeeper's family members also worked in the shop.

TELEGRAM BOYS

In the first half of the 1900s, most people did not have phones. To speedily pass on urgent news, they sent a printed message called a telegram.

The message was delivered by a telegram boy. The young men who did this work were usually teenagers.

Sometimes a telegram contained happy news. Often the news was devastating.

During World Wars I and II, families dreaded seeing a telegram boy at their door. The message could be that a loved one, who was away fighting, had been killed!

Telegram

Telegram boy

How did telegrams work?

The sender went to a post office, wrote out their message and paid. → A post office worker sent off the message electronically using a telegraph machine. → The message travelled from telegraph office to telegraph office until it reached its destination in Britain or another country.

This telegram from August 1955 contains happy news!

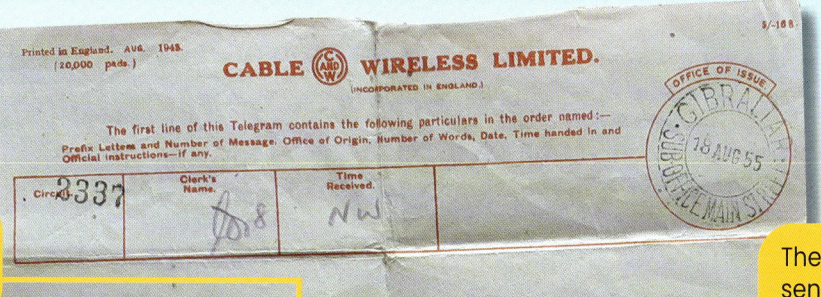

- The message was sent from a post office in Kent.
- A teleprinter printed the message on thin strips of sticky paper.
- The message is just nine words long because every word cost money.
- The message was sent to a soldier, Lance Corporal Phillip Owen.
- The destination was an army barracks in Gibraltar, in Europe.
- The message was sent by the soldier's mother.

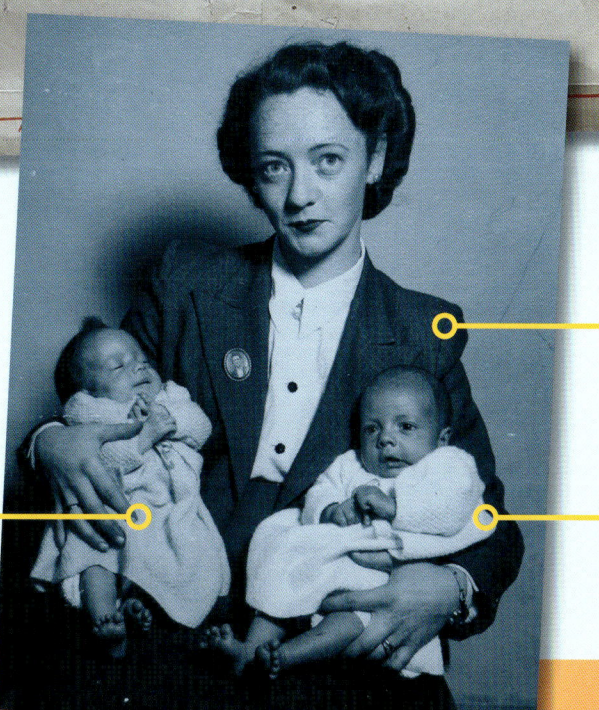

- Evelyn Owen (the soldier's wife)
- Jenny
- Steven

➤ At the destination post office or telegraph office, the message was printed and put in an envelope.

➤ A telegram boy delivered the message on foot or riding a bicycle or motorbike.

➤ A letter could take days or weeks to arrive. But a telegram could pass on news in less than an hour!

NUMBER, PLEASE!

When people first used telephones, it was not possible to just ring another person's number.

Instead, when you picked up your telephone, you were immediately connected to a worker called an operator at your local **telephone exchange**.

"Number, please," the operator would say. You gave the operator your phone number and the number you wanted to call.

To connect you, the operator removed and inserted jack plugs into a switchboard. If the call was local, she connected your phone line directly to the other person's phone.

An operator wore a headset

Brenda (Born 1941)

"At my **job interview**, I had to do a hearing test and read out loud so they could check my voice sounded clear and polite. I also did a spelling test. I remember spelling - apologise, particular and search. Most telephone operators were women. We were faster than men at making the connections on a switchboard!"

To make a long-distance call, an operator connected to an operator in another town or city. The call might be passed along a chain of operators at different exchanges until it could be connected.

Switchboard

Operator

Jack plug

Grace (Born 1933)

" We had to neatly write a ticket for each call we connected. It showed the caller's phone number, the number they called and the length of the call. The tickets were used to calculate the price of the call so it could be added to the caller's phone bill. "

MAKING WORDS

Today, we **typeset**, or type, the words in a book, magazine or newspaper using a computer program.

Before there were computers, typesetting was done by people called compositors.

A compositor was given some text to typeset. Each word was created using tiny metal letters that were placed in a composing stick.

So that the text would print the right way around, the metal letters were back to front. The compositor also had to create the words upside down!

Composing stick

Small metal spacers were put between each word.

The metal letters were known as "sorts".

The sentences were placed into a metal tray that would become a page.

Compositor

Information for typesetting

Tray

Metal letters

Metal printing plate

The typeset page was used to make a solid metal printing plate. The plate was put onto a roller in a printing machine. It was covered with ink and then rolled and pressed against paper, again and again.

RAG-AND-BONE MEN

Just as we do today, people in the past recycled. The unwanted items they saved were collected by a rag-and-bone man.

Riding on a horse and cart, a rag-and-bone man rang a bell and shouted, "rag and bone" or "any old iron". People brought him the items they wanted to throw away and he sold them.

Brass bell

A rag-and-bone man in the early 1980s

Scrap metal

Metal could be sold to a scrapyard, where it was recycled to make new things.

Glass jars were sold to jam or pickle factories.

Leftover meat bones were sold to factories that made soap or glue.

A rag-and-bone man in the 1950s

Rags

Unwanted clothes in good condition could be sold at a market. Scruffy, old clothes and other rags were sold as stuffing for mattresses. They could also be sold to factories as cloths that workers used to wipe their hands.

HOLD VERY TIGHT, PLEASE!

If you'd travelled on a bus before the 1980s, you would have met a bus conductor.

In those days, passengers boarded a bus and found a seat before paying.

Once everyone was safely onboard, *Ding Ding*, the conductor rang a bell twice to tell the driver to move on.

Next, the conductor had to find the newly boarded passengers who still needed to pay.

The conductor walked up and down the moving bus, collecting the passengers' fares and printing out tickets.

A conductor shouted, "Hold very tight, please!"

Passengers in a queue